Airplane Graveyard

poems by

Bryce Johle

Finishing Line Press
Georgetown, Kentucky

Airplane Graveyard

ACKNOWLEDGMENTS

Thank you to the editors of the journals where some of these poems first
appeared:

Maudlin House: "How to Fix Transistor Radios and Printed Circuits"
OneArt: A Journal of Poetry: "A Short Game of Catch, Then Back to Bed"
The Hedge Apple: "Late Night Texts While My Brother and I Argue," "Quality
Time," and "Week One," published as "Marriage, Week One."

I wouldn't have all these poems without Sharayah, my wife, who pushed me
to start using my gift again.
Gratitude is owed to Caleb James Knoedler, my cousin-in-law and fellow
writer, who helped me put this manuscript together and reads all my good
and bad writing more than anyone should ever have to.
I am indebted to my college professors, Jeffrey Voccola and Claire
McQuerry, for guiding me in my writing journey.
Lastly, thank you to anyone else who has helped me along the way but has
not been mentioned in this space. You are all important to the process and
the world.

Publisher: Leah Huete de Maines
Editor: Christen Kincaid
Cover Art: Sharayah Fanning
Author Photo: Sharayah Fanning
Cover Design: Elizabeth Maines McCleavy

Order online: www.finishinglinepress.com
             also available on amazon.com

Author inquiries and mail orders:
Finishing Line Press
PO Box 1626
Georgetown, Kentucky 40324
USA

Contents

For Sharayah, who hears my stories

Relocation Management

The company will reimburse a man's flight
to the wrong place
only a few hours' difference

Not only is fare to Tampa less expensive
and non-stop, but his father lives there,
whom he will visit
                              for two days

before driving to Melbourne for work
in his rental car with unlimited miles
thinking infinitely   of Father

                                        I wonder what that's like.

The complexity of releasing texts
for car advice like the small toads
I caught with pride just yesterday

He responds with Agent Orange payloads
in all caps, and between the nonsense,
I read his top baldness and cancer of the ears,

printouts on self-diagnosing depression
forgotten in the paper tray
for his eighteen-year-old son to find

I moved away to college
then I moved away to work,
away with defoliated wisdom
just not too far   from the auto shop.

The Rototiller

In my parents' garage, the rototiller,
caked with soil and dead grass.

There's a picture of Dad struggling with it,
the meat in his arms and cheeks rippling
in constant tremor waves
watching the windmill blades
burrow into the earth roughly,
but I fear it's a vaporous one.

Our garden, where he used to spray
glittering sparks on the tomatoes,
I was more interested in the intricacies
of the indoors: paisley print on my bedding,
coolness of our food supply in the fridge,
shape of the controller in my hands.

He marked me down.
That spells *lazy* over the roar,
the reigned animal engine
he toiled through stale dirt.
Though, you probably aren't strong enough,
anyway.

In my professor's office, his old reading chair.
When I sat, the leather groaned like packed snow,
and I had to look upward to meet him.
You're a worker, he told me,
and he has a lot of kids, too.

One day I wrote him a letter,
a thank you note for removing my collar,
and then I shut my eyes,
pulled a book from my shelf,
and sowed its heart.

Quality Time

Dad didn't get it

when I sent him a letter
asking him to guide me through
repairing my mother-in-law's old radio,

rather,

he told me to bring it to the wedding,
he'd take it home with him,
fix it in six to eight weeks.

Takes a lot of knowhow,

equipment, requires good soldering
skills and WHAT to troubleshoot.
Must know knowledge of circuitry
of solid state and vacuum tubes;

Electronics is NOT easy.

Under the covers with my wife,
I wonder if I'm meant to try again
or let him dwindle day by day, clueless

in his bedful of acquired tools and parts,
keeping them for himself.

Baby's Room

Office,
my small space,
must be renamed

without a raise
affording another room
in a lawless part of town.

From velvet touch of my writing chair,
gravity sucked away
and the feet of books in shelf,

Telecaster and its amplifier
floating, prescient from wall and floor
agreeing to a broken physical law

when we think up a child,
where it will go,
like breathing, crying furniture,

unless neither of us
can peer into swished old vine
Zin like crystal ball

to find the legs to build one.
Then this space, this office,
can keep its name.

How to Hold Him

Wally's body writhes
  Tongue rattles out
Long, dry slug rolled

  up against whiskers
His silent snout
  clouded, frozen eyes

My father's best
  The perfect son
was without words

  Bed of rot
our dead dog
  and Dad's spirit

rocked in staling air
  my arm, his back
Consoling, I guess—

  something never taught.
He had a great life...
  My mother said.

Psychic, she and I
  collided thoughts in the fog
while he wept

  (What about me?)
We wouldn't dare
  Not today.

The day I first saw
  my father's tears
    didn't know what to do.

Growing My Own

A black chain link fence around this decorative garden,
    where a mind could be like sin, chipped blue temptations,
        peach of pastel, hard metal thrones empty under thorned
            wrought iron arches. A land to rule

of grass burn and plant decay. This is our neighbor's backyard,
    and bones cropped from my mental forest trail, where I am
        when I tell Ray my dream of drawing tears
            instead of nightmare sweat

when my youth pastor's cancer returned. The cold church rooms
    come back with that old chartreuse couch, our names
        scratched in the armrests: *Zack, Zeb, Jesus, GOD.*
            We should've carved Ron, role model.

If I'd just gotten to know him. Or knew to try when I was young,
    knew that I needed it while Dad was laid up in bed
    with back pain on morphine, or violently dry heaving
            through pig esophagus when he forgot.

Is it too late? Is that why funerals are following Ray everywhere,
    and why my chest keeps itching lately? I try paying
    no attention to the misshapen mole in my skin. Probably
            nothing. But still, *Ron. Endings.*

Doctor says this is not the end, but GOD's hint to mend slack
    strings in my heart, to tie the Gordian knot which only I
    can undo, to till and tuck seeds inside and bury it to affect
            this desolate space with manhood.

And granted, my garden has always been home
    to spade, hoe, rake, waste cans—items ignored,
        inherited for creation, for planting perennial morals, sprouts
        like field horsetail

that tell me when the soil needs
loosened.

I can raise them for myself
and call them *father*.

Coffee Table

Wood pallet
Bonding favor
From father-in-law

Pry it apart
Crowbar, hammer
Unnail

New tools
Drill and bits
Hand-me-down table saw

Ripping—ejected plank
Rocket
Into back door

New fear
Broken ribs
Punctured stomach

Friend shepherds arms
Two from one, safely
Scored character, glue edges

Composite
Pine, ash
Finely sanded

I assemble myself
Zinc screws, liquid plastic
Plugging pockmarks

Slicking pigment
Mahogany shade
and oil shield

New surface
Living room fixture
To swallow spills

My diverse veins
Tunneling knots
For manhood

One day a desk
With covered table
And bottomless, buoyant drawers

One day a house
Insulated, elephant hide
Supple door, warm maple syrup inside.

Our Wedding is in Six Days and We're Binging Gilmore Girls

You're scooping fruit and date filling onto dough
I'm flexing my abs and biceps my first time through
Little pockets bubble in the middle when you fold it

because you still need to bake and sell
your homemade vegan Pop-Tarts and next to cinnamon brown sugar
wedding cake is the reigning favorite flavor lately

since your customers purchase the artist
your supreme wisdom surrounding spring, fall, your mother,
when love can be learned in transitions, books of leaves and foul petals

You're pulling the spoon trigger to release sweet paste
while Lorelai and Rory endure their boy vicissitudes
You hope my mouth ends up in a movie one day

reminiscing on the calming tone my vocal cords emit:
Remember when we didn't used to have sex and now we do?
Your mouth belongs in a movie too:

Can you believe you lost your virginity to me?
Two to three seconds in the truth of it
and then the false of it pops like a clown balloon

Wedding cake has wild berry filling (you worry, being eight years apart)
and cuddles under the blankets with non-dairy buttercream
After you fold the dough into little pockets
you're crimping the edges with a baby fork your child used to feed from
and part of me wishes she was ours
or since I'm yours I could bake my own treat to share

Crack my knuckles (you worry)
Mold your dough with my fingers and form a hollow pouch
Dollop the seedy puree and pipe in the silk

Top with frosting
Cool
Test for taste; feel for kicks

How to Fix Transistor Radios and Printed Circuits

He plops down a faded blue hardcover book
and says when he dies,
this has all we need to know.

This will tell you about the electronics and
engineering of transistor radios and
how I fixed them, how they hold their value
so read this and learn.

I'll keep them under the bed, stored safely
in Ziplock freezer bags and Sterilite boxes
preserved until they're ready for you.
Then when I'm gone I want you to go on eBay.

Don't just get rid of them,
use some discernment in regard to
what other people are selling
and price them appropriately

so all my work doesn't go to waste
and I can leave you with some money
when I'm burned or buried.

A Short Game of Catch, Then Back to Bed

We played catch once
with the baseball mitt I got
when Mom and I were movie extras
in our little Pennsylvania town.
You taught me how to throw

straight up sky high, keeping
my eye on the ball, and catch
my own pitch. That way, even if
you aren't here because your back
and mind ache and it's just me,

beside my forgettable forty-eight
frames of fame, I can still practice.

Airplane Graveyard

You keep dismantled wings
of remote-control airplanes
in the rafters of the garage.
You say some might still work
but who could know?

You say they can't fly any longer
because nowadays they cause
interference with commercial jets
and I believe you as a boy,
                                         but not so much anymore.

What would really happen to us
should we reattach those wings
and motors, fill the gas, and lift them
into the air?
                           A guess:
we would freeze up in knowing
I never learned how to land,
and you'd fear these

balsa wood toys would be
destroyed along with the post-war
childhood you invented for yourself
to cope with coming home.
                           Not to worry, they're still up there
               hung like the poorly buried dead.

Zoom Reunion, 2020

Name your favorite childhood Christmas.
I stand up from the couch,
leave my brother and fiancé
and myself, walking through canker sores
like little painful stars, confused wounds.
I grip the short spade kept by the bed,
an invisible fist around my own,
and in the yard, I dig.
First layer yields grass and dirt.
Second gives me nightcrawlers,
a blank list, unwrapping plastic BBs.
Third layer is frozen solid, transparent ice,
Buzz Lightyear and Woody, acoustic guitar.
We had doughnuts every Christmas morning,
Dad brushed his teeth, made the bed,
brewed coffee, sounding yawns while we waited.
Gifts, not memories. Traditions routines.
Fourth exhales behind my ear from birth,
like one screw drilling into another,
snapping in half just before flush with ash,
I'm always almost on my earth.
It draws me back, still life with cut wires.

Dad was a Heavy Machine-Gunner in Vietnam

We're calling it ash, white ash near Dad's garden, property lines,
    and I can't recall its species,
so we're calling it ash
             since that's how memory goes.
Heads and arms squirmed outer leaves like beetles on broccoli
    when my older brothers climbed for snagged frisbees,
wiffle balls, foam rockets
             and paratroopers.
By the garage, and the deck Dad built, apple tree.
    I climbed this one, water-rifling family picnics aloft
like smiting brothers, who nailed wood rungs and platform
             in its boughs.
Dad warned of ticks year after year, 'til ash was leveled to trunk.
    I still played war in trimmings with the boy two doors down,
hiding his antique rifles, his rucksack, and   ourselves
             from the enemy.
We twisted ankles on hard and sour immatures nestled greenly.
    I drew their stems with my teeth and tossed them like grenades
until our neighbor
             chopped apple down.
The boy geared in his Pop's drabs to find a new scouting tower,
        a younger apple tree in his own yard,
and our game   resumed
             from branches,
where he spotted the enemy once more, and rappelled, rope
             knotted over naval.
             Bark burned by tautened braid salted the roots
as he went wide-eyed   pendulum, dangly oversized boots,
             breath punched, hissing free.
Dying, he begged for mother, so I ran. *He hung himself*
    from the apple tree! This mother coughed smoke
with steak knife, to find him giving up fast   suspended like
             a spineless marionette.
She hoisted his butt, irritably sawed the noose, and set him
    down, confiscating the remains for our safety
as he contemplated   in dirt
             his whole 9 years—his future children.

Later that summer, we caught a squirrel in a chipmunk trap.
    Quiet air felt like it eavesdropped on our crime, as its tail,
bloody cartilage wreathed in the door   springs,
                    entombed him.
We were tired   with horror
                    on heat-swollen hands   beating for dusk,
    when my kid brain knows that big, leveled tree
                    as Silver Maple,
and we shyly sought help   like in war again,
                    from someone else's Father.

The Weight of Guns and Eyes

Our couch, a stop away from home
to rest a bad back and shiny knees
swollen amidst the big being out of town.

Subconscious clockwork, plans to avoid
contact in the eyes like nervous strangers,
hurrying time through the cushions.

Our restaurant, *what is this, a menu?*
What is this, Mexican food?
Just have what I'm having, already,

and have you read the signs in this place?
I'm reading, I've never been here before—
Ah, twenty-one or older to drink, it says.

Our wedding, a corner chair to be apart, save
knee pain, to look at the rims of his glasses,
poke at his living will with his phone finger

instead of dancing with his wife, excusing
his tie to gander at the blimp passing over his shoulder,
our eyes repelled like north on north, south on south.

Our home, should an intruder barge in,
will survive us, if the garden shovel I swing
for protection fails to draw blood.

I'm unfamiliar with the weight of my father's guns
or our temperatures before and after fire,
but I will look the stranger in the eyes when I go in swinging.

A High of Eighty-eight

Two of us on the front page
of the Williamsport Sun-Gazette,
Braving the Heat.
Packs hitched to hip
like utility belts, accoutrements
loaded for survival: fluids, rags
for hydration and wiping bullets
so our eyes don't sting
walking our neighborhood.
Past my elementary school,
down to K-Mart,
and home again.

Don't look at the camera,
the paper man said,
but I did—and still am—un-candid and I'm thinking
of war films I've avoided
inspired by acts of my walking buddy
and all the other victims of conscription.
Dad collected them on VHS.
In obsolescence, he stole them
from the internet, burned them
to disc because he's done his time
and they are his,
despite the absence of his own young face
muscling kill machines on screen.

His drooping chin perched high,
a chicken peaceful, head intact
beneath grayed mustache and bifocals.
He sips a can of Diet Pepsi,
favoring his cane.

No one like John Rambo ever lived,
but he and his little blonde boy
in patriotic visor
rough sand sweat and swamp ass

while everyone else fears the inferior
mirage melting streets.

Not us. Father and son rivaling
Pennsylvania humidity,
making it together,
fame without bloodshed.

Chemtrails

Sometimes I wonder if I'm remembering all wrong
the things you never did, how tired, how much pain
you were in, so much that you couldn't be as good
as we needed you to be.

Then sometimes I wonder if it's just me, and
your other sons don't care a lick about moments
like the ones I wish I had but don't and never will,
and time is funny,

hindsight seems to bring you clarity, but it's more like
since past is past, I have a hold on it like leashed dogs
and can bend it to my will. Which presents a problem
and once again I wonder

if I'm blaming you for me becoming the characters
I've played, when it's really just fate trickling down
from chemtrails and infecting my internal narration
like straw-stuffed metaphors

egging on family conflict. Sometimes I wonder, but
really, I doubt that's it.

Beasts No More

Cheap plastic toys are blown by wind.
Once arranged neatly by old children, they
topple in sand, hollow molds filled with grit like marrow.

An Aztec Temple, miniature, abandoned,
army men and millipedes scatter in gutters,
catch in desert weeds and black plastic tatters,

and after another storm, they vanish.
Then one day, ages later, this rubber dinosaur,
this lost plaything reappears. This red-gray behemoth

finally finding way. Under sand, he digs
out the old temple again, and it's mostly intact.
His people are inside and jostled, eroded

by the whirlwind that twisted through,
but they still act like same old, same old
army men and millipedes following orders

from factories where they were born.
Yet, the rubber beast comes home
with new iron in his guts, his brutish snarl

retuned for prayer and licking wounds;
he knows to build, he's got to tear
the castle down, so he does it, removing

one plank and letting sand run, bury
up to Adam's apples, the chins of his family.
He'll stand aside, and watch them shake off

head to toe, learning by the ants
and worms, crawling and squirming
grains—it's swimming in sin,

how their old model cars and seashell
troves are the end all be all, along
with programmed television.

He is a brother whose dino spines have grown,
garnered plasticity for his siblings to squeeze
and contort the purpose of fangs, stretch thin

scaley flesh, and he howls at the moon,
which isn't something dinosaurs do,
but he does it out of pride and the pain

of resuscitated DNA. Think repaired hope,
turning powder into glass for bridling electricity
across a reborn territory.

Occasionally, his brothers show small sparks,
cracked acorn caps that fall from the sky—
the invocation of a tree whistle in mind.

Best Man

O, the dreadfulness of public speaking,
you, brother, moaned months ago.
Tore me down over special words
in vows and time capsules.

When time came,
I expected something primitive,
simple, done.
Your voice quivered incompletely,
but as you primed,
the whole barn sparkled, globe lights
strung across
reinforced beams and joists.

See, now? Isn't there pleasure
in giving yourself?
Your first funny poem
read aloud to announce
my bride's taking
of our unpronounceable last name,
and the grateful end
of your reluctant speech.

Tennis Elbow, a Gift from My Nephew

The state of my right arm is that it throbs.
We just *had* to arm wrestle at my wedding

when I was half drunk.
You beat me at Christmas,

you little cheat,
but this was *my* day.

We stationed our elbows on the tablecloth
and clapped as we linked hands.

None of this shit, and with my other hand
I straightened your hooked wrist

and put you right back
where you belong, evened field.

We both struggled and groaned, except
now I'm aching and worrying about getting old,

but I am invincible, my mental body is
resilient, overcomes foreboding thirties talk,

as I'm observed by the sheen of your gray-circled eyes
peering at me under long, shaggy high school hair.

When people ask about you, your gnarled mouth,
your tests of strength, I suggest you're frightened,

planning parricide while miserably holding out
for your long-distance love.

You're too young for that, I say,
wincing in pain, a win under my belt.

Late Night Texts from Mom While My Brother and I Argue

Her neck nods, then halts, catching herself from sleep
on the couch, like when she'd come home from work
while we were under her roof

I feel like I need to fix something
Blue light flickers into the wrinkles of her sixties,
into her cheeks and eyes

Or that I failed somehow
I feel bad you guys aren't friends
And now she takes misguided grandchildren

prays for them to iron out and keep straight
their young souls, which my oldest brother wasn't
taught how to mold. So she tucks them in sleeping bags

and takes them to church, and does the old job
that three-verse number of hers
and one day they still strangle a cat

or kill one in the dryer when nobody's looking
or run away from home
or sneak out of the detergent aisle to be alive elsewhere

but she knows it is an eternal role
her Earthly purpose, to be mother and half father:
to love unconditionally and to scrutinize

a lack of common sense
to make us tough and sweet like the Fraser
fir-shaped sand tarts she bakes at Christmas

You didn't fail us, I say, picturing Dad's nest of tools,
all the work he's done for his collection of transistor radios
You had to be more than you when Dad gave up…

We're friends, I assure. *Just different people.*
Yeah, she says. *Dad does seem like that.*
But he's so proud of you.

Week One

My Ukrainian wedding band:
a strip of wood, a sample of lichen,
forest hues hardened in resin

I tend to tense my fingers
below knuckles, stiffening,
tendons kissing hard,

an obsessive squeeze for release
which brings the fear, inadvertently,
I'll crush the ring in time,

freeing foreign vegetation
from my promised finger,
stasis to alien air

I chose this one for its floating greens,
a primordial reminder
where we come,

but I know nothing of
the creator's home
or the war down the road

How could I?
How could you,
from here?
If anyone should ask,
it is a frozen wheel of the planet
that made us, our trembling, affectionate guts,

a chain of mushrooms, leaves, and pumpkin sun,
offerings of a morning after rest, reminders
of turning renewable soil,

finding lovely sameness,
unbreakable cellular repetition,
clean cancer for the soul.

Come from War

I am tender for the M60,
the combat knife they put in
your hands to kill
when you were seventeen

It's strange history,
you were married once before,
had kids with someone else
besides Mom. I forget sometimes

I have half-brothers and
don't know half of it,
stories of your life, who you used
to be in high school, before

How you became the man
glued to the bed and spooning
more with the dog than my mother,
rewinding Vietnam in its inflated
directions and nightmares,

who still, at seventy-four,
ducks and cowers in fear
at the gunshot of a produce bag
bubbled and popped.
Tender and sorry,

they drafted the senses
from your nerves to become soldier
child, a little less human,
and left you to your own
to dig yourself a sloppy hole after the end;

your mother jettisoned
nearly every piece of paraphernalia
and would have burned your memories
if she could. Stuffing years

of terror in compact layers
like a knapsack to be shipped
off-world, along with

addictive, simultaneous nostalgia
That era longed for in instinct,
you must look back on true gore,
buddies asking for *mama* one last time
Too much, too long to block it out,
so I know it's not completely your fault

your heart is unstable, prone to fragmenting
like old live grenades saved in a shoe box,
stagnating in a closet,
you couldn't teach me to pitch them
with natural strategy

like you would have
if adulthood, as you entered it,
was more than learning how
not to die, how
to get normal and loved
in your own country,
your home.

Without those lessons on weaponry,
I find I don't know how
to talk or forgive you
for all the untold past
furtively flowing through my blood

But I am tender for who you could have been
were you allowed to embrace
the real man
when battle commanded its own
grisly masculinity.

And while I'd have to go to war myself
to truly understand, I can see
your eyes wanting focus on a raindrop
through our pollen-stained window
The reflective one on the telephone line
way across the street.
But they just   can't
make the shift.

Pointing the Bricks

These days I try to be a house,
feel as old and sturdy as possible.
A well-crafted antique to exist
while it rains and the smell of worms
travels in small gusts
and gusts travel through us. Houses.

Strong as we are, we develop cavities,
simple erosion of time and weather.
It gets me up at seven thirty,
the jackhammering into my pores.
They say they scrape out the old,
then add fresh mortar around our red brick.

As a house, I wonder if it's normal
to get that sick feeling, the headache
from rainy days and no exercise.
I wonder if it's okay to have rain-sadness,
or if I'm making architectural associations
about calamitous precipitation and the cost of repairs.

Maybe I'm being human.
Maybe I'm being an animal.
Maybe I'm not a hundred-year-old house.

Bryce Johle holds a degree in Professional Writing from Kutztown University of Pennsylvania, where he was a two-time winner of the Karen Blomain Award in Fiction, and also the recipient of the Bennett Harris Humorous Writing Award. He is a co-host for the podcast, Arcade Bookshop, which discusses the literary qualities of video games and their textual counterparts. He practices Krav Maga, Taekwondo, and kickboxing. His poems have appeared in publications such as *Parentheses Journal, Eunoia Review, October Hill Magazine, Maudlin House, Rabid Oak, and Pennsylvania Bard's Western PA Poetry Anthology 2023*, among others. Originally from Williamsport, PA, he now lives in Pittsburgh, PA with his wife, Sharayah, and his stepdaughter, Genevieve.